MW00992439

I Was Somebody Before This....
By: Kitti Jones

ISBN-13:978-1979063975

ACKNOWLEDGMENTS

Thank you to my siblings Kristy, Sylvia and my best friend and my only brother Bobby White! My dearest and best friend Latoya and her mother Joyce. De Angela and Ken Davis, my road dog Henry and most of all the loves of my life Chris and Kellian!! Without the love and support of all of you I wouldn't have gotten the inspiration and strength to write this- Thank you

Table of Contents:

Dedicated to: My mother Deborah Anderson you're my hero and the strongest woman I know in this life! - Your daughter

The experiences and details are true. Some names and details have been changed or obscured to protect the identities of individuals.

Chapter 1
Little Did They Know

I was eight years old when my mom moved me and my siblings to Texas, my mother was a strong-willed independent woman who sometimes made bad choices in men but she didn't waste time leaving when she had enough of the bullshit! The week before moving to Texas we had packed our bags in the home I was growing up in, in Kansas City, and while my step dad was away, we made a fast getaway down a trail that led to a busy intersection, my mom hoping the neighbors didn't see. As we ran across the street the wind hitting my face was like fresh air, and I just felt relieved leaving that house. My mom had been abused and she was finally leaving this time and she had bigger plans for us. A week later we were living in Dallas-Fort Worth with a family friend and eventually we moved into our own house, my mom was beautiful and young with three kids, new in town, and the men were noticing fast! She was hard working and stayed to herself. I admired my mom she didn't like to party and never took drugs. She worked as a nurse and made sure we had our essential needs. She remarried again and we lived a happy life.

As I became a teenager I thought back to those days before moving to Texas and wondered if I would ever be faced with an abusive man that I loved? I told myself that if I did, I planned on killing him if he put his hands on me! Those were my exact thoughts as a 13 year old, reminiscing about my younger childhood and the things I saw. Around this time I was heavy into listening to music in my bedroom waiting for my favorite songs to come on the radio so I could record them, Guy, New Edition, rap music was heavy on radio and I would pretend I was the radio dj introducing the songs and my brother and cousins would act like we were performing on a stage. It was the best fun.

In 8th grade we had to write a paper on what we wanted to be when we grew up and I said, I wanted to be an actress, and the class laughed, including the teacher. I was a middle child always trying to make sure I was seen and heard so I loved going to drama class and participating in everything that made me feel free and allowed me to be expressive. My teacher instructed me to pick something else like the other kids and to read it the next day in front of the classroom. I was fighting back tears because everyone thought it was funny, it was humiliating, but it was then that I realized that the environment in which I lived in, the dreams I had were too

big and out of reach for them to imagine.
Most people in the area were content with
just being able to get by week to week,
paying bills from jobs they hated.
Everyone seemed to just be existing and
not living.
I returned to school with a new paper, to
satisfy the teacher and class, saying that I
wanted to be involved in politics instead,
hoping it would get an A , at that time I
didn't know what the hell politics meant
exactly, I just read a long definition for it
and piggybacked from there. I knew it
sounded good for a grade, so I did it to
satisfy my teacher. I didn't want anyone to
laugh at me. But I planned to get the last
laugh little did they know...I saw the
laughter as motivation to prove everyone
wrong. I just knew there was another life
out there, and this couldn't be all there
was.

Chapter 2
Acting Class, Video sets, and Soul Train

Late 90s early 2000s I was in my early twenties and living in California. I had gotten married and an opportunity to live in the LA area for my spouses job was presented. I didn't know a lot of people, a few distant family members but that's all. That summer after spending months adjusting to a new city as a new wife and mother, to cheer myself up I attended an R. Kelly concert and was first in line for my ticket to purchase, no one I knew wanted to go with me, I didn't care. I loved his music , his style, and how he seemed so oblivious to what people thought of him . I didn't like concerts but he was my favorite artist and he didn't just sing he put on a damn good show! The concert was amazing. I was on third row screaming my ass off, the TP2 album was the hot album at the time and he was the biggest R&B artist that everyone wanted to see, be around, and work with. I left the concert happy! I got my thrills and that man had a spell on the women in the crowd including me, it was worth the 90$, I thought.

In better spirits I decided to take advantage of my time in LA and pursue my dream of being on stage. I didn't have any acting experience at all but I was ambitious and didn't take no for answer. Around this time having a computer was a must, most things you needed were beginning to be a click away and this is how I started searching for the perfect agent to represent me in LA as an actress, and this is also where I found my first acting classes. I looked up my favorite actors on IMDB to see who was representing them and from there I wrote down the numbers and called trying to get an appointment, one agent Jerry Pace said to call him in a few days , he may have an open appointment, Yes! Progress, I thought. I found a guy online by the name of Ivan Markota he had a list of actors like Sherri Shepard and a few up and coming actors that he trained under his techniques and I wanted to see what he was all about. I called him over the phone and he set up a meeting first. I met with him in his office on Hollywood Blvd. and he liked me right away, told me his fees, and told me when classes started. I didn't join right away but my husband was supportive of my dreams at the time and agreed to get a nanny while I went to class.

August of 2001 I was finally in class and new students were introducing themselves, one young girl stood up with her mother and her best friend and stated that she was almost 18 and that she was in class because she wanted to be a star. She said, Jada Pinkett was her favorite, and that she loved Barbara Streisand. Two years later I would see the same girl as New New in the movie ATL. I didn't stick around in his class long, I did meet people that suggested I network at some events and find ways to earn my union card. I ran into well know actress who was also an acting coach who gave me information on her classes at the West Angeles Church on Saturday's and I was ecstatic! I couldn't believe it, she had connections, and was working with big tv shows at the time on the UPN channel like The Parkers. With having her on my resume now as my acting coach, I went back to looking for an agent. I called back Jerry Pace of Zanuck, Passon, Pace their roster was almost entirely experienced actors, but I didn't let that stop me. I went up to his office dressed like I belonged and the receptionist said Jerry Pace doesn't have you down for an appointment, let me call him up to the front for you. I got scared (armpits started sweating) it's looked down upon to just walk into offices with no invite or scheduled meeting. I played it cool as he walked to the front lobby and I said "Hi Jerry Pace , I'm Kitti we spoke last week? I'm still attending acting classes and looking for representation. I just left the set and wanted to speak with you before I went home for the evening?" He says " Well normally I would've been home already for the day, but sure, come on back to my office," motioning his hand to follow him. Jerry was a older Jewish man, gray beard, not a lot of hair left, wore glasses and he was very laid back and believed in me right away. He did ask me "Why should I represent someone with no work yet", I said, "because someone believed in you before when you hadn't worked yet, and I wouldn't be wasting my time here if I didn't believe in myself? I'm asking you to please take a chance on me.

He reached out his hand to shake mine and said "thank you for coming I'll give you a call". I stood up and thanked him and walked through the lobby to my car and started crying !!!!! Did I just make an ass of myself ? He had the most unreadable expression on his face and I just didn't know how he felt about my answer, was I too arrogant? I was still trying to think positive but overthinking at the same time. As I drove home I convinced myself that either way it was a boost of confidence and I was definitely determined to be taken seriously! I walked in the house and my husband notified me of a missed call less than five minutes ago from Jerry Pace asking if I could call back at 9am the next day because he was going home for the evening. I could not believe it, he called me!! Wow!! I started overthinking again. OK, if he didn't want me he wouldn't call to say he didn't want me , would he? It was the worse sleep waiting on 9am to come the next morning. I called, he wanted me. That's all I needed to hear.

In my acting class, our coach attracted a lot of celebrities, cast members from The Parkers, Lizzie McGuire, and some well known video vixens were in my class too. This was " the" person to have on your resume at the time and I felt good learning from her and her male assistant . I wasn't as good as the others yet, but I wasn't giving up! No way! My first gig was an extra on the video set for JaRule "Down ass Bitch." I wore an orange jumpsuit and got my first taste of long hours, little pay, and cold pizza. I didn't like this, I thought no more videos for me. My next opportunity was to dance on Soul Train during the time Shemar Moore was the host. When I walked into the Soul Train set it felt surreal. I grew up watching this show on Saturday mornings excited about my favorite celebrities performing here and my crush then, and still was, R.Kelly. He had performed there in the early 90s I was a teen so in love with him and his songs were so beautiful like Dedicated, Honey

Love, and Seems like You're Ready. I was at Soul Train, I thought again. I was about to dance and was hoping I was going to be chosen as a scrabble board contestant, I laughed inside . Life's good, I thought back to my old class in 8th grade laughing at me and just smiled, I wish they knew that laughing motivated me.

Soul Train began filming Heather Headley , India Arie, and Robin Thicke (when his hair was long hair) were all there performing. It was like a dream come true and it was then that I realized that everything I wanted bad enough, I was going to get! Acting class and having my agent allowed me to get on sets as an extra for The Parkers, General Hospital (a waitress), Lizzie McGuire , Half And Half, and an audition for Cheetah Girls (yes the nerve of me thinking I could sing) it was a fail for me but it eventually became a huge group for Disney. I was building my resume with these small roles, attending classes, networking, and I was focused, nothing or no one was going to slow me down, I thought.

Chapter 3
I See You using your voice- For Something Else.

The reason I was drawn to my acting coach the most during my years in LA was because she genuinely loved what she did and her students, she wasn't sugar coating anything either, if you were horrible she would tell you and make you get it right! She was a Godly woman too and her spirit felt warm. One day after class she pulled me to the side and said , "You've been coming here almost a year. You've come a long way and I want you to keep working on your techniques; but I strongly see you using your voice for something big, something else. I am not sure what, but it just came to me. " I didn't know what she was referring to yet but just two months later the broadcast bug had bitten me while I relocated back to Texas and I immediately began networking to get on the radio.

My husband and I bought a home back in Dallas and I started pursuing radio full force. No experience, just like I entered the acting business, but I was confident and wasn't going to let anyone tell me NO.

I put a resume together after volunteering at a Christian station at an AM channel to learn about the equipment and the lingo. I asked a lot of questions, got coffee, and filed papers but it was just what I needed. I then went to drop off my resume at KLUV in Dallas, at the time they had a network for the Dallas Cowboys and were hiring promo girls, they picked me.

I lasted at KLUV about 3-5months, before I quit. I knew what I wanted. I had the experience I needed and I was ready to hit the bigger stations in town!

There were only couple big hip-hop stations in town, one of them was newer and had more down to earth people that I could relate to, hoping one day I would be apart of their team. One night at a big convention I introduced myself to a "big name" guy in radio, at the time, and he was attracted to me, he didn't care that I was interested in learning the radio business from him, we never again talked business, he wanted to know when he could see me in private . He was handsome and everybody wanted a piece of him. I was warned, but I fell for him even though I was still married. During the affair, I had already filed divorce, not as a result of the affair, but we were approaching our ten year mark married and I was so young when we married not knowing a thing about love plus we had only known each other six weeks and got married and by now he was living in Italy, and I refused to go with him. I wasn't focused on radio at this time, I wasn't working at all. I spent too much time doing the wrong shit with the wrong person! With the divorce pending and my 3 year affair at an end in 2006 I regained focus on myself and my goals. From somewhere my ambition returned, that fearless person who first stepped into that agents office in L.A five years prior. I felt like the go getter I once was again and vowed to NEVER let another man or relationship make me lose my focus on my goals, and who I am again! It wouldn't be long before I ran into someone who told me that 97.9 The Beat was hiring and that I should interview if I still was interested in doing radio. I walked into the station with the interview scheduled, and nailed it! The PD at the time suggested that if I was serious about starting out on the air instead of promotions street team he wanted to see me tomorrow training with the Midday person at 10am.

Well…I showed up at 7am!!! I meant business.

I had all day to learn the boards, equipment, commercial logging, vox pro, and how to record call-ins. I did not leave the station until 17 hours later at midnight, needless to say the PD was impressed.

I trained for four days straight, and that Saturday he put me on the air for the first time at 9am. I remember it like yesterday. Ludacris and Young Jeezy "Grew Up A Screw Up" was going off and I started saying, "Aye that was Luda and Jeezy grew up a screw up…"....I froze. Nothing would come out of my mouth!!! I stared at the mic and couldn't move! Suddenly, I hear running and it's my boss coming up the stairs and he bursts into the studio and presses the button to take it to

commercials. I was so embarrassed, all
that confidence and training and the first
break to talk on the air I blow it! My boss
was positive about it, reassuring me that
people in their cars, and at home on
weekends are not worried about that
mistake, and that I can make it up on my
next break to talk. A pep talk was all I
needed and I finished the next two hours
without issues, nervous but not freaking
out live on the radio. I got through my first
day and he decided to have me on the air
every weekend overnight for more
practice. Each Monday he would go over
the mistakes I made and coach me on the
things I could improve on and the good
choices I made as well. I always had a
notebook writing down everything he said
and suggested, he loved that about me. I
was new, very open to criticism and open
to being coached because I was looking to
establish a serious career. Although I had
gotten a settlement in the divorce, I didn't
want to spend it all and be left with
nothing. For three months I worked

weekends, and then suddenly a major slot opened up
at our station at night 10p-2am. There were people who were sending in resumes from everywhere, Dallas Radio is market number 5 and being on radio in this market was a big deal. Internally people who worked weekends like me and others who wanted to be considered for this position had been at the station longer than me and felt they deserved it. I never put my name in the hat for it because I didn't think I was seasoned enough to take over a slot, which was held by a guy who was number one all the time, those were big shoes to fill. So I thought .

After a month of watching everyone wait to see who he was going to choose , he picked me, and heads rolled!!!! I signed a two year contract with a one year option. Base salary, plus bonuses for hitting number one or two in the ratings. Rumors were flying that we must've had sex or that he was trying to get in my panties by giving it to me. People weren't so nice to me anymore. I started being bullied by a few girls who did weekends on radio and ran promotions, they knew the nightclub scene, and knew how to help me get my name out there to represent the station and to get me paid for my time. It soon got back to me that they hated me, and started spreading disgusting rumors to promoters about how I got my job to make them not like me. I was being sabotaged! Or atleast they were attempting to although the promoters still liked me and hired me for nightclubs. I was still floored when one promoter told me all this had been happening. Floored thinking why are they setting me up to fail ? Why?

I quickly learned that if you're a female with success you are a " Bitch or a Hoe" people will make you into one of the two . It's not your skill, education, charm, ambition, or your marketable look, you "had" to get everything that made you a success with sex, is what they say. I went through hell after I got that position, one girl on staff and her sister tried to fight me at an event the station was having accusing me of saying I didn't like them, it was childish, and the wrong place to confront me even if I had said it? They were written up and fired a few months later, "allegedly" for stealing. They hated me for my come up and so did a few others. Still I loved my job but I knew karma would handle the ones that spread nasty false rumors, at some point and if you believe in karma it definitely came for many.

Chapter 4
Middays and Married

I was so happy that I had gotten past my first two and a half years on radio and most of the negative vibes were fired or quit. I was always number one in my slot and I had a lot of fans of my 10pm- 2am show. I came up with this segment called "freaky tales" and listeners would call in and tell me about the sexual acts they were about to have and I would entertain them with my commentary. This became so popular that I was the first person to be considered when our midday position opened up at the station, that would now put me on the air at 10am-2pm in the daytime! I immediately had on-air ad sponsors and partnerships with major companies! No one could tell me shit. I was arrogant as hell by now, I had the clothes, the shoes, and the car. I always looked well put together. But just as things took off for me professionally my love life was fucked up yet again. I had gotten engaged to a guy, I started losing myself again, gaining weight, not liking to go to work because he was jealous, we had purchased a new home together, and after three months of living together I left. Again, I said to myself, every time I let a fucking guy in my space I become unfocused. I moved out, got a condo and focused on winning at work. I dated guys who were with me because of who I was, the look of it, or wanted their music on the radio. I peeped game fast with those type.

I dated guys who had no ulterior motives as well, but nobody stood out and I just wasn't trying to let anyone get me off track again.

Soon I met an ex NFL player. Not long after seeing me he asked me on a date, I said no, he smiled and said girl take my card. I took it. We met up at a restaurant two days later. He was the life of the room, everyone was jocking him. I liked it, confident men were a turn on for me, I loved his confidence and I hated having to play myself down with the previous guys I had dated that were insecure with the attention I got from being a radio personality. I thought, ok he fits my type. After dinner and drinks he walks me to my car and shoves his tongue in my mouth without even asking! I wasn't a drinker and he didn't have the freshest breath so I said no baby a hug for now. Yuck! We hugged and he begged to hang out again that weekend for Super Bowl. I agreed....

It had been snowing bad and events were canceling left and right! I wasn't about to drive my Mercedes I paid cash for and wreck it in the snow to see this fool. He agreed to send a car service to come pick me up. When I arrived he hugged and kissed me made sure I saw he was driving a Bentley and led me into an exclusive sushi spot and told me "baby after this let's go to the strip club". While in the restaurant his male friend arrived and they went to the restroom together, I didn't think anything about it. Seeing he had invited someone I called a girlfriend of mine to join me and she was in the area and came inside. My date kept going to the restroom during the hour and a half we spent there and was full of energy ready to continue partying all night! I didn't know what he was doing so much in the bathroom, I figured maybe he was another scummy ball player who has a woman he has to check in with?

Again I didn't know why he was so energetic and he was ten years older than me, whatever, I thought. He and I get in his car and my girlfriend follows us, with his male friend to the strip club. My friend and his friend go into the club before us and while we waited in his car he starts asking me to lean my seat back so he could give me oral sex. I thought it would be sexy so I let him. It wasn't even good. He then opened his glove compartment and had something inside of a sunglass case and sniffed it. I wasn't sure at first if it was cocaine until he tried to shove it up my nose! He held my neck against the head rest while my seat was still reclined and with so much strength from his hands press on my neck he said "take a deep breath". I tried to say no but he was squeezing my neck and I had no choice but to sniff. It was powder cocaine. I felt light headed and sweaty after that. I don't recall everything after that moment except waking up furious in a hotel with him and telling him to never contact me again! I felt taken advantage of and I threatened to report him. He kept calling me apologizing, then admitted to me he was married and wanted out of the situation and that he'd been doing things he probably shouldn't because of the pressure he's under. I was furious with him, so I'm thinking on top of all this you're married too motherfucka?! I hadn't taken drugs in my whole life, not even marijuana and I rarely would have a margarita back then. I saw what drugs and alcohol did to people in my family and I was not about to let this fucker turn me into a dope fiend or his mistress ! He started wooing me, afraid I would tell, bringing me gifts at work, even money once when he saw me out shopping. I didn't want anything to do with his crazy cocaine habits or him so I changed my number and moved on with life. All this time I had imagined what I would do if a man tried anything with me, thoughts of that 13 year old promising to protect herself against any man but I just wanted to pretend he never happened. So I did.

Chapter: 5
Call me Daddy:

It's summer of 2011 music is blasting in the studio at the radio station! I'm dancing and flipping my hair to a throwback R.Kelly song "Fiesta" I cannot wait because his concert is tonight in Dallas and I'm giving away third row seats to caller 9.

I never missed an R.Kelly concert and I was always in good seats and on time! I needed the fun, my weight had picked up a little from work stress and the guy I was seeing a professional business man a few months, turned out to have slept with at least two other women at the station I worked for, and I'm the last to know! On top of it, I find out he'd been seriously seeing someone else at least for nine months! I'm so pissed…because a few people knew we had been hanging out and he had even come to the station and helped me write a few commercial spots for my show. He was a great catch. I dug him a lot and to find out others knew that he wasn't who he was presenting himself to me, really embarrassed me.

One day I was recording a spot while he sat in the engineering booth and a girl that worked in another department at the time who allegedly did a lot of sleeping around with the guys in that department kept walking by the engineering window looking in. Let's call her Tina. Tina waited until he and I walked out and she proceeded to speak with him in the lobby area as I walked back into the booth to finish my radio shift for the day, there was a glass window and I could see them. Tina appeared to be aggressively talking and he just stood there in a calm demeanor replying but I could not hear what was being said by either of them. I didn't think much of it at the time . But she walked away abruptly.

There was also a woman whose job was to greet guests, everyone stops and talks to her, especially celebrity guests, while they waited in the radio station lobby to be called back, so, she learned a little about everyone over the years like… who was dating who, who was getting fired, who was being interviewed , what celebrities were on the way, and I too sometimes shared with her while standing in the lobby some "girl talk". On one occasion she asked if I was seeing " him" (the businessman) I said, "yes" and I told her how amazing our sex life was and explained how he held nothing back with me and I even showed her a few text he sent gushing over what happened one evening as we went to strip clubs, dinner and had wild sex! She listened with a smile, loved every minute of the tea I was spilling. I asked her if she was seeing someone and she said, "I was a few months ago but he had an issue with me asking him for a favor" and she mentioned him not being an "oral sex giver ". I replied to her...No girl! you did right by cutting him off." I leave the station for the day my phone rings and it's him calling, he doesn't sound too excited in his voice so I asked "what's wrong"? and he proceeds to tell me that Tina (from another department) was trying to threaten him with telling me they hooked up and he told her to fuck off and that he would tell me himself ! I was floored! He proceeded to say it happened All Star weekend (which was in Dallas that year), that she was drunk and he drove her home because she couldn't drive and during the drive she performed oral sex on him. He said he was not interested in Tina that she was not his type of woman and he didn't get aroused. He also confessed to me that he and the girl who greets guest (yes,the one I had just giggled and had girl talk with about him) had sex, and he wasn't interested in her further and that it was way before me, almost a year.

I was driving listening to all this in shock, and somehow I made it home. Not remembering any stop signs, lights, exiting the freeway or anything. I was just home safe but in shock. Things with him were not the same but I kept seeing him because I didn't feel like trying with anyone else but I was still hurting, he didn't know.

So, Here I am it's R.Kelly concert night and I just got a call to host the official after party. This was going to be an epic night for me! I had to skip the actual concert to be on time to host the after party. I tell my radio listeners where I will be hosting and how they needed to be in the building to meet the king of R&B with me.

It's 1:25am and I'm at the club downtown in Fort Worth waiting for R.Kelly to show up, and suddenly his tour bus is coming down the one way street, my heart started to beat a mile a minute. I was used to meeting celebrities, interviewing them, and doing meet and greets. At this moment, no one was as legendary as him except the time I met Scarface a rap legend and Will Smith.

The DJ announced his arrival and I made my way over to his designated V.I.P area. He was taller than I thought. He was more handsome in person and he had so much charisma. I introduced myself, "Hi I'm Kitti from the station the host tonight." We shook hands and I asked for a picture for the radio station website . He agreed flirtatiously and we posed quickly for the camera. I hated the picture and wanted to retake it but I didn't want to be "that person". I said to him "I heard from hanging on Twitter that the show was amazing. I hate I missed it" he replied, " You see one you've seen them all." I tell him it's not true and that he is very creative in each show and that I never miss them until tonight. He suggested I come see him in his next city since I missed it. I said sure "I'd love to come/cum that would be great", slyly smiling knowing he got the point. I was being naughty and he liked it. He stared in my eyes almost hypnotizing me with this look of sex. I broke the stare, trying to remember I was at a work event and remain professional, but it was hard!! I adored this man for a long time! I need to get away and get my shit together so I tell him I'm going to the restroom for a second, and he says "no don't go yet, shake my hand." I look at him with a flattered reaction but confused as to why we should shake hands again. He sticks his hand out and I shake slowly while giggling.

Suddenly I feel paper and he says "Don't look at it yet. Text me when you get in the bathroom". I get to the bathroom in shock and without thinking twice I text him, "Hi, R.Kelly this is Kitti you said to text you…" he replied,

"Good girl. Save the number. But always call me Daddy ".

I left the bathroom almost in a panic. I went to get the money that was owed to me for hosting and I immediately went home without saying goodbye to him or anyone for that matter. I look at my phone and he is calling me. I answer nervously "Hello?" "How old are you?" he asked, I replied "I'm thirty-three", "Well you don't look no 33." he said. Wasting no time, he dived right in, "When can you come see Daddy? " I said, "On weekends I'm off from the station." He said that he would have his runner set up a date for me to choose what city I wanted to visit him on tour, but before hanging up he says, "Baby always call me Daddy."

(Rob and I June 2011)

Chapter: 6
Are You getting peed on?

It's mid July and my birthday had just gone by. He missed it but sent me flowers that week and an edible arrangement, but no text or a call in almost 3 weeks. We had exchanged texts and photos often after we met and then he disappeared. I didn't worry too much. I was still having seeing the "business guy" but much more casually and immersed myself in my career. I opened up the blogs for the day and jotted down my notes for my radio show and saw news that R.Kelly had cancelled his remaining tour dates. I immediately text him and said that I hoped he was ok and he called back whispering to me that he had just made it past throat surgery and he was sick. As soon as he got better he wanted me to come to him.

I told him ok and to take it easy, I missed talking to him, and that I'll send his assistant my vacation timeframes. He replied " OK send Daddy some pics everyday ok," I replied, "OK I can do that Daddy." At this point I realized he just loved being called "Daddy" but to me he was just Rob.

Finally, I get to see him again. It is the last week of August 2011. I met up with Rob in Denver. I had only planned to be in Denver until Sunday morning because I had promised someone at the radio station I would fill in late afternoon for them on Sunday. The best way to describe the encounter is just bizarre and confusing. He had me in a separate hotel room but same floor because I made it to Denver before his tour bus got there, and his assistant booked my room. While waiting in my room I put my bags away, I ordered food, I took a shower, and I waited. My cellphone rings and it's him. He says he is on his tour bus two hours away, asked me if I had eaten, and wanted to make sure I was OK. He then requested I send him a nude pic, I said "OK" and he corrected me and said, "It's , ok Daddy." and I said " "OK Daddy I will." I sent him ass photos and full nudes asking if he was going to taste me. From his replied I could tell he was getting very excited. An hour passes by and I hear a knock. I look through the peep hole and he's standing there in an Adidas sweat suit. I quickly open the door. He plopped down on the sofa and immediately pulls out his penis masturbating, I asked, "Would you like for me to do that for you Daddy?" he replied " No. Just walk back and forth in your panties." I'm thinking, ok I'm into freaky things.. but this was different. As I modeled for him his moans got louder and louder. He instructed me to sit reverse cowgirl style on his face, demanded I that smother him going from anal to vagina in pleasuring me. I asked him if I could do anything for him and he said "Not yet. I have to teach you how to be with me. Let me control this." He then proceeded to direct me to arch my back while he watched himself in the mirror please me more and specified how he wanted my leg to be bent. Confused, I did what he asked. He complimented me on how clean I was and to always be that way for him when we have sex. Once he makes himself ejaculate we talk and he asks if he can take a few photos of me in my underwear and to which I agreed.

That weekend was both exciting and bizarre for m., I finally had my private time with someone I grew up having a crush on. Admiring his talents and the mysticism he had about himself. After our encounter he spoke with me about visiting him in Chicago after an Africa trip and I agreed to it. He then went down the hall to his private room where he said he will be up all night recording ideas and having meetings. He asked me if I wanted food, to order what I wanted, and to find a mall for the next day. That next day he had a driver take me to a mall where I purchased makeup, a Prada handbag, and a pair of gold Prada shoes. After I returned from shopping, I thanked him, "Thank you Daddy" I said. Pleased I remembered to call him daddy he kissed me. A very passionate slow kiss. One that gave the most euphoric feeling of lust and intrigue. Over lunch, I learned how funny Rob was. He started telling me jokes that would start out as serious stories and by the end there's a joke behind it. I remember slapping his arm for getting me all emotional and it wasn't real. We laughed so much,I didn't want it to end but I told him my flight was leaving at 6pm. He insisted, "No don't go yet. I'll have my assistant change your flight!" I said "Oh no I have to be at work tomorrow on the air." Sitting me on his lap he said "Call in for Daddy tell them you have a flight issue. I got you if they trip." He looked so sincere about wanting my company and needing my energy around him. I made the call and spent another night in Denver.

After I returned to Dallas, I get a call from him expressing how much he enjoyed me and that he wanted me to accompany him to Africa in a week. So ecstatic and overjoyed with my new feelings for him, I told him I would love to go but I didn't think I could take off work in such a short notice and for an entire week at that. Saddened by my declining to put work aside for him, he said he understood and requested I send him photos everyday and that he will fly me to Chicago when he gets back!

I went to work with the biggest smile and I had the biggest secret. I was dating R. Kelly! He was crazy about me and I was falling hard for him. I wasn't open to telling just anyone about us only a handful of close friends and two people at the radio station. I didn't want anyone questioning my professionalism since I met him at a work event and I wanted to respect Rob's privacy as well.

As weeks of communication continued with Rob and me flying to see him in Chicago, every other weekend, I started to notice strange behavior from his runners, engineers, and assistants. No one would look at me and say hello or acknowledge I was in the room at all.

I always arrived to his home or studio before he did when I flew in town. I would be waiting for a couple of hours at minimum for his arrival. He would text me, and check on me, letting me know he was on his way and telling me that K (one of his runners) will be bringing me food or something to drink and just let him know what I would like. One particular visit, I text Rob that I wanted food from a popular Italian pizza spot downtown Chicago (which was less than a mile from where we were). Rob arrived finally. He then told the runner, "Go get food from there. Make sure there's enough for everyone and here's the money." Approximately an hour later, the runner arrives with pasta, sandwiches, cheesecake, tiramisu, salads, and utensils. Rob stood up, looked at the spread on the table and began yelling at the runner for being "the only idiot he knows that will go to a pizza place and come back with everything they have BUT a fucking pizza." The room broke out in laughter, but I felt extremely embarrassed for K as he stood there turning red and acknowledging his mistake. He offered to go get pizza to please " Mr. Kelly" and expressed how sorry he was.

This incident was the first of many where I was able to see how he treated his staff and how they went to great lengths to please him regardless of how he treated them. I knew after my first few visits that people were afraid of him. They depended on him. They ratted each other out to please him. He ran a tight ship. Full of people who wanted his approval and would do anything to gain it!

It was now the second week of October 2011. I'm on the radio airwaves giving away Chris Brown tickets. During this time I was falling In love with Robert Kelly. He was everything you want from a guy. He was sweet, he was romantic, he was consistent, he made time for me. He would send flowers to me at work, call me every day and express how much he wished I lived in Chicago.

He made me feel special and needed. It made me feel sad that I wasn't available for him.

I found out from Rob that the same woman who was my acting coach in LA, that I adored so much, was the exact lady that discovered him in the late 80s. It just felt more than coincidence that we were connected this way. He met her in Chicago and I had met her nearly 12 years later in L.A. Our chemistry was already amazing and we felt this connection made us even closer.

By this point I became very protective over my blossoming relationship with him. Rumors started to spread that I was flying to see R.Kelly on weekends throughout the radio station. One afternoon I logged onto my Facebook while I was playing songs on the radio posting promos for my followers, when I received an inbox message from a fake page who wrote :

"Are you going to get peed on this weekend?"

Wow. Just fucking wow. I immediately wanted to cry but I was at work and all I could do was just be angry, delete, and block the person. Only a few close friends and my coworkers knew of him and I, so I immediately thought it had to be someone at the station. This was just the beginning of the sadness I started to feel working at the radio station during this time. People were talking behind my back <u>again</u> and I felt uncomfortable.

Chapter 7
Next time you come ...you gotta stay!

By the end of October I had officially fallen in love with Rob whom I called Daddy. He had shared things with me including his molestation as a child, his mom dying, his girlfriend drowning and dying , people close to him stealing from him and taking advantage of the fact they knew he couldn't read well or write.

I didn't like hearing negative things about him anymore and I didn't partake in any gossip regarding his past. I especially didn't like conversation with people trying to ask me if I was dating him or mentioning the infamous sex tape. I felt such closeness to the man that the public was still joking about over the trial he had been acquitted over. Comedians and celebrities would mention him in songs from time to time poking fun.

During studio sessions I would sit on his lap and listen to him direct the engineering. At this time he had been recruited to do the soundtrack to the movie remake of Sparkle. I felt special. I was hearing songs put together no one knew of yet. I was listening to him speak about how he didn't like one of the actresses voices for a particular song but how it may work out anyways . Also during this month Rob was starting to go on trial for another incident involving a former mentor that claimed Rob and some friends allegedly dragged him down a flight of stairs and beat him over a disagreement over money and credit for a song.

One morning while I was visiting he woke me up and said he will be back around 2pm and that after court we will go shopping and to dinner. He was wearing a suit. He smelled amazing. As he went to leave he ordered me to stand up and hug him. He said to start standing every time he walks in the room and to greet him with a kiss. I said "OK Daddy. I'm praying for you in court today and I love you."

When he returned, I remembered to stand up, kiss him, hug him, and compliment him. I told him I prayed and things will work in his favor. He gave me a look as if he was pleased with me. He liked that I knew the exact things to say and what to do to make him happy. Around this time we had sex several times throughout the day when I would visit. It wasn't excessive in my eyes because we didn't see each other enough.

I remember us making love after he came from court and it was the most perfect and normal time because it didn't require all the extras that later came with his sex life, it was just us. We didn't use condoms, he trusted me and I trusted him. Sex with him was passionate during these visits he was still directing me a lot but I found a way to not be offended and I understood what his turn-ons were. My visit was almost over it was time to fly back to Dallas and get back to my reality and my radio career. I felt sad and couldn't hide it. He saw I was sad and said, "The next time you come here you gotta stay baby girl." We hugged. I tried to lay on his shoulder so he didn't see my eyes water and watched one of his puppies named Snow jump around on him .

I hadn't thought over the last four months of the possibility of me leaving what I knew to full time live in Chicago with him. My heart started beating fast, wow, what would that be like? At home, it was boring. I spent most of my time when I wasn't working alone as my son had the opportunity to live abroad with my ex-husband. I was definitely all about work and living for weekends to visit Rob at this point so the thought of feeling this love and togetherness with him permanently was something to consider. I eventually looked up and asked him, "What about my job and my car and my place?" He said, "I will give you all that and pay you double what they are paying you at work. But you gotta live here man. This is gonna get old". "I have friends here, female friends that live here," he said, "that I want you to meet. But I want to make sure you are ready for it cause some girls can't handle it and they don't last." He grabs my chin to kiss me and says, "Are you ok with everything Daddy do?"

"Yes Daddy."

"Do you love Daddy?"

"Yes I do."

"Well make me happy and come be with me your family can visit, it don't matter."

I started crying, I never felt this type of love in my adult life. My marriage lasted ten years but we had only dated six weeks before getting married It was rushed and we were completely different people. We lasted so long because we ignored the truth until I was the one to say, let's end this and live our lives.

Being with Rob made me feel like I was dating someone I didn't have to figure out. It wasn't about the trips or gifts. It was about our connection. My ex-husband was romantic, we took trips, he made a great living and provided me with luxurious things so it wasn't an issue. Rob was different. Up until him the guys I was involved with weren't very forthcoming with who they were and hid important things about themselves that didn't allow me a fair chance to decide if I wanted to be involved before falling for them. Rob was open about who he was. What he liked, his desires, his dislikes. This was "the one" and I left for my flight back to Dallas 75% sure I was going to give up my life to be in Chicago with R.Kelly.

By the time Halloween rolled around of 2011 I sold my Mercedes, paid up a few bills, and saved the rest. I was packing and sending boxes to Chicago and making plans to quit the radio station the next week.

I was terrified it was the last step in proving to him I was loyal and wanted this relationship as much as he did.

Rumors of my planned departure started to erupt at the radio station and my male colleagues started avoiding talking to me and even avoided making eye contact. We had just gotten an new PD and he wasn't working in the office yet, so there was another co-worker who was in charge until the change was complete. He treated me really bad, not giving me heads up on promotions or places I was scheduled to be. I overheard him calling me a "dumb bitch" to the girl running the promotion staff at the time and I just became more and more uncomfortable being there. I always think back and say to myself if the environment was a happy one at work and people weren't harassing me with fake social media accounts about dating R.Kelly it wouldn't have been a question to stay or leave. I felt like an outcast. With all I had endured over the five years, on the inside, I was tired! I was being disrespected. Even though I had a top show my radio contracts weren't offering the money that reflected my work and the previous PD started constantly berating me and harassing other employees (he got fired a month before I quit) all this is going through my head and I was ready for a new chapter and a new life!

It was on a Sunday November 6, 2011 . I was interviewing Diggy Simmons. I don't recall much about the interview because the main thing that kept replaying in my head was how was about to send this email to resign from my position. I had just signed on for another two years under contract, but the contract was insulting. I thought after the five years I've spent at the radio station proving myself? I was trying to convince myself this place didn't deserve me. All I knew was that I had just sold my car, packed some boxes, ship some things, and the last thing to do was to quit my job after this interview! As soon as it wrapped up I sent an email stating that I was resigning from my position due to some family issues. I thanked them and I sent a tweet saying that I was onto my next chapter! Here it was again…my heart racing! Everyone was staring at me as if they knew that quickly that I sent that email. I made eye contact with a coworker who was in charge at the time as I was walking out the building. He didn't say anything to me. Finally when I got in the car I started crying right in the parking lot. Not because of anyone's reaction, but because I just walked away from something I worked so hard to keep and I knew that my life was about to change in a major way.

The fear was haunting me of the unknown …. the next morning I would be off to Chicago.

Chapter 8

She looks a lot like the girl from that sex tape!

It's November 7, 2011. I remember arriving with my bags. I had already sent boxes and I remember sitting in Rob's downtown studio waiting on him to arrive. It was 8 o'clock at night. All I kept thinking was Wow!! I did it!! I'm here! It's wintertime and I officially live in Chicago now! Is this a dream? I quit my job, I sold my car, and although I still have my apartment in Dallas for another three months (the lease wasn't up), besides my savings it was the only security in the back of my mind. Overall, I was excited I was there. Rob expressed how pleased he was with my decision and he couldn't wait to see me.

Another hour went by.

Another hour and another hour

It was a little past midnight and no Rob!

I started to panic he knew I was moving here today. We talked about this! I thought. I just spoke to him this morning! Does he actually know the hell I went through to get to this moment?! What the fuck is he doing having me sit here?! He had me waiting five hours for him to arrive.

He instructed that I go straight to the studio from the airport and I sat there just waiting. Right before 1:00 AM he walks in. I stand up immediately because by then I knew to stand up when he walked in the room, kiss him, and compliment him. I immediately forgot how angry I was becoming because his presence always took over me, I hugged him and I kissed him! I did exactly what I knew he wanted. I thought he would act a little bit more excited that I was finally there for good. He told me to change my clothes because we're going to go to the basketball court. Late at night an old church would allow him and his friends to play on their court. I changed my clothes into sweats and he gave me a few minutes to meet him downstairs. We got on his tour bus and had oral sex with each other and then we arrive.

While walking to the basketball court he instructs me to sit on a bench by myself. I noticed everyone else was on the other side. I was sitting cheering for him and then suddenly another girl walks in and sits next to me. She starts cheering for him too, clapping each time he made a basket. She then says hello. I remember thinking, she's pretty, but I wonder if she's here for him. Is this a fan? Why is she sitting next to me and not where everyone else is sitting? All these questions and insecurities going through my head after I fly here, wait for hours, and now this. We continue to watch Rob play basketball for the next hour. He won. He was very aggressive on the court, it was impressive, he demanded respect, and I admit his confidence on the court was sexy. He cursed guys out and I could tell in some instances they just let him have his way. But he was really talented on the basketball court. Quickly after the game ended he walked over to me hugged and kissed me, then hugged the other girl and kissed her on the forehead. I looked at him very surprised. Rob said to her "introduce yourself" and she reached out her hand

and said "Hi my name is Sheila nice to meet you.", I replied "Hi my name is Kitti, nice to meet you." Rob then says, "OK good, now that that's out of the way, let's go to the dressing room". While in the dressing room, I notice he's very comfortable being naked in front of her and he proceeds to change his clothes in the open and joke around with us both then asks what food we wanted to eat. I said I didn't care. Rob suggested a popular soul food place that catered earlier, and stated he would have one of his assistants warm the food when we got back to the studio. Rob planned to work at least until about six in the morning. The three of us got on his tour bus to go back to the studio. She began whispering something in his ear I see him nodding and then he whispered something back in her ear. Shortly afterwards, she left and got in her car which was parked in front of the bus. Whatever they said, she decided not to ride back with us to the studio, and I was glad. I didn't know her, I didn't know what role she played in his life. I also just couldn't shake the feeling I had seen her before.

My first two weeks were amazing, just like when I would visit. There were times I didn't see him for almost the whole day because he would be working, traveling, or at least I thought he was until I learned different later. I knew he had kids and he was divorced and he would spend time with them. I saw them but I wasn't introduced to them.

Thanksgiving was coming up soon and I wanted to spend it back in Dallas with my family and my friends. He agreed that it would be a good thing for me because he was going to be traveling shortly as well. There was a new vocal talent show on tv and they were having him perform with one of the finalists. I went back to Dallas happy to see everyone, even though it hadn't even been a month. While I was visiting a friend had asked, "Hey with you being you in radio did you ever run across R.Kelly's sextape?" I immediately became defensive and furious towards my friend why was she bringing up something that he had been accused of and acquitted of years ago?!

How dare she try to ruin my happiness!

How dare she try to put that in my head that he was a bad person!

I hung up the phone on her and it kept going through my mind how I hadn't seen it before. I saw images, still shots, still frames, but I never actually watched it. At this point my curiosity got the best of me and I searched the internet. As soon as I typed the search query I saw images and I was stunned! I started shaking. I go ahead and click a link for the video and begin to watch. I can feel myself wanting to cry because the more I started watching it, the more I realized that the girl that I had seen sitting with me at the basketball court a week or two before look a lot like the girl in the tape! At this moment I feel really dizzy. I couldn't stop crying. I didn't know what I walked into! Is he the monster everyone says he is? If this is the same person, even if she wasn't under age, she's been around for way longer than me! He's invested way more in this person. Does he love her? Are they secretly in love? Are they hiding it from everybody? Why am I around? What role do I play? I just gave up my life and he had the audacity to introduce me to her?! What the fuck did I just get myself into? What the fuck have I discovered?

I immediately call him and I'm crying the first thing he says is are they fucking with you?! He was thinking people were going to bother me about him on my trip. I said. "No Daddy someone told me to click on a link." I lied I didn't want him to know I searched for the tape and said, "it was a sex tape with you and when I seen it, it resembles Sheila." He became furious yelling at me telling me I was a stupid bitch, to don't ever get in his business again, and let people tell me things about him, negative things, and that I needed to get on the first flight back to Chicago the next day!

I did as he asked and went back immediately. When I got in the car from arriving at the airport I got in the backseat and he began slapping me over and over again telling me how I was a stupid bitch, stay out of his fucking business, I pleaded with him to stop I told him how sorry I was and that I would never do it again, I thought the more I cried he would stop, but it didn't work, he was angrier. I told him that I didn't believe it was him in the tape that somebody sent it to me to look at! I'm sorry Daddy! (I kept saying)… hoping It would make him stop and he kept slapping and kicking me, fussing , and making sure I got the point! It was the first time he laid into me and made sure I wouldn't forget what would happen if I ever ask him about anything negative or rumors regarding him. I got his point... and that was the beginning of me being afraid. I saw the fear of the staff he had at the time, and others around him, now it was sinking in. I laid in his lap crying while the car drove home. We had dinner and shopped the next day. We never discussed the tape again.

I should've gone back home immediately. but I didn't want him to think that I would tell his secrets for money and abandon him for money like others had. I was in and I was in deep. I vowed to kill a mother fucker at 13 years old if a man did hit me! And I let him live. I had never let a man call me out of my name and get away with it. Was I allowing it because it was R.Kelly? I knew things that the public didn't know about him, I was protective over him I didn't want people to know, that I knew his secrets. I've never had this kind of connection with anybody on any level, he was so open, and so was I, no guards were up, all defenses were down! I let him be himself and with that came everything. More than I bargained for.

Chapter 9
Dimming My Light

Happy New Year!! It is 2012, birthday parties back to back in January. It was Rob's birthday month he was turning 45. I loved him. That's all I could think about when I looked at him! He started getting offers to host All-Star weekend's, Super Bowl's, and this was around the second time he had introduced me to Sheila. But when I saw Sheila for the second time I tried to forget I saw the tape. We played card games. We laughed.

Rob proceeded to tell me that he wanted me to meet the other girls but he wanted to make sure again that I was mentally ready.

What I didn't know was that with all the small instructions and wishes he had been giving me about my dress and behavior towards him he had been slowly shaping me into this person that mimicked all the other women in his life that I didn't know about at the time. I was dressing in baggy clothes, I wasn't allowed to go and cook my own food. Someone had to bring food to me, or I had to wait until he was awake and ask what we were eating. He was uncomfortable with me or anyone walking freely throughout his studio or his home. You had to knock before opening every door. Runners would pass him small notes all day so people in the room didn't know what they needed to tell him. I also had to ask to go to the restroom. I later learned this is because he didn't want me to discover any other girls by crossing paths on my way to the restroom. Everyone had to ask so he knew who was going and who was coming, so there wouldn't be any running into each other. I didn't realize this was the reason for the rules. I just followed them. I wanted to make him happy.

Rob seemed very happy when Sheila would come around. I watched them play fight. It bothered me, but I understood. I don't know why, I just understood. He would ask her how her mom was doing, he also asked if she wanted to go with us to Aruba it was coming up in a couple of months. She said yes.

Sheila stayed for a little while and later left. That night was the first night Rob introduced me to another sex act that I'd never performed on a man… ever…

He wanted to be anally stimulated and pleasured with a sex toy he had in a bag.

I remember, thoughts in my head were… I can't believe he's into this type of freaky shit!!! I didn't like the idea and thought damn, will I look at him differently after this? Maybe. But I still loved him and I was happy with him being comfortable with me, so I did it.

I watched and listened to how much he enjoyed it, he moaned and groaned until he ejaculated. I felt like I had this power over him to make him feel like that, he told me he wasn't comfortable with sharing that with anyone, only me, and because he's built up that trust with me. He swore I would be the only person that he would ever share something like that with.

He told me loved me, and **I was never going anywhere**.

Although it was uncomfortable to watch him enjoy me doing this to him I still loved him and I wanted to please him. Whatever it took.

That was the beginning of him showing me another side of sex that I had never seen.

Valentines Day rolled around, gifts, fun, love, excitement, traveling, and then I was dropped back off in Chicago later that week because a famous friend of his in the music business had died and he was asked to sing at her funeral. By this time, I deleted all my social media but I reactivated my Twitter account just so I could watch people's reactions to him singing at her funeral. He had done such a marvelous job. People were applauding him, he was trending. I was proud of him. At the same time I snuck out a tweet and people wanted to make sure I was OK immediately because they hadn't heard from me in a while. I wasn't checking in with people as much and there were others that didn't think he was actually my boyfriend. Many thought I had gotten fired from the radio station and I moved to Chicago lying about being with him. But of all the many rumors were going around I was just happy nobody knew the control that started, the beating over the tape, or anything negative.

After he returned from the funeral I got a beating for not telling him that I walked to CVS. It was barely 2 blocks away from the studio! Rob would sleep during the day and I knew the runners would probably try to rest when he rested because of his demands. I don't know what I was thinking, I guess I felt terrible having to ask someone else to get feminine products for me. When I got back it was probably one of the worst beatings because it seemed like it lasted forever. Hitting me over and over and saying, "You don't know anybody in this fucking city. Anything could've happened to you. You don't leave without telling somebody or asking! You didn't even text me! What if something happened to you and I can't explain it? You're being a stupid bitch! I can't have stupid bitches around! I got too much to lose!" I went back to my mindset in the car and again and again kept apologizing until he stopped slapping me around.

By March 2012, it was four months into being in Chicago. I had lost at least 10 pounds and was at best 120lbs. I started feeling depressed because of the beatings. I started lying to my friends and family making them think we were having a good time. I would make excuses about why I wasn't talking to them and tell them we were traveling a lot and that's the reason I couldn't call and talk to them as much. They were happy for me and I had the chip on my shoulders to prove to people that were doubting my relationship.

My old radio job was mentioning me on the air making fun of me. I was saddened by this. There were rumors about Rob allowing one of his houses to go into foreclosure. The morning radio show where I used to work reported on the foreclosure and then proceeded to say "well we know someone who used to work here who might be coming back to Dallas homeless with a backpack." Everyone on the show burst into laughter! I had gotten emails and calls and it hurt me so bad I cried in the closet, hiding. Rob noticed that I was upset and I shared with him what happened he had warned me people would attack us for being together and was upset for me. It didn't stop, a total of about three more times in the year of 2012 I was made fun of on the radio by my former colleagues and it was humiliating and embarrassing. All I kept thinking was if I leave this situation and I want to go back into radio I can't! Everyone knows, everyone's going to judge me, people are laughing at me, no one respects me.

At the onset of my heavy depression Rob started immersing himself in the studio trying to release an album that spring. He put the album out, it did well, but not like his others.

He started to hate when I would mention anything about my radio career or any accomplishments that I had in the past like appearing on Soul Train as a dancer, the Parkers as an extra, and Half and Half. He would say, "Did I asked you about all that? Stop trying to get attention it's not about you it's about me!" More incidents of him being irritated easily caused me to be slapped here and there. I ran off once and spent time in Atlanta with a friend when I wanted to get away from him for a little time. It wasn't long before Rob came to Atlanta looking for me. He thought I was gone for good and in an attempt to win me back asked me to go on tour with him and be apart of the show in a skit feature. I didn't know what he meant because from what I could tell he didn't like me getting attention or talking about myself but I could tell it was an effort to repair what was damaged.

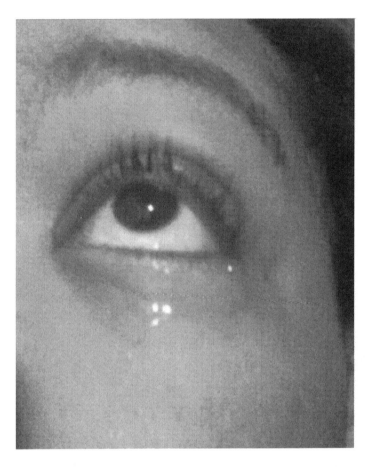

As I look back now I realize he was dimming my light from the time I moved in. Making me wear what he wanted me to wear. Eat when he wanted me to. Talk to just him or friends he introduced me to. My head had to be down when men walked by. I had to stand when he walked in the

(Bruised eye spring of 2012)

room. I had to constantly compliment him, laugh at his jokes only, and tell him how great his music was, and practically agree with all of his opinions.

My light was dimmed. He knew Atlanta was a sign I was wearing thin of it all.

He promised me change and this tour will repair things because we could travel for two months together. I will be part of the show, and he will pay me for the cage skit as well. He was letting me shine and I was ecstatic and ready to tell everyone about the Single Ladies Tour !!!

Chapter 10
I raised them..

Yes! Things are feeling like they did a year ago. Maybe he was stressed over the last album or constant things in the press. Especially now that his ex was on tv doing reality shows, it had more people criticizing him. I was going to make sure I didn't do anything to upset him now that things are back on track and people will "see us together" as he put it!

I was on a flight from Atlanta to Columbia,SC for rehearsal to kick off the first night of the Single Ladies Tour. I arrived with a driver waiting and taking me straight to rehearsal where Rob had been all day he saw me and started explaining how he wanted this cage skit to go. First he had a wardrobe girl practice the skit before I had arrived so I could pick up how he wanted it to go. I watched the two of them practice it twice and on my first try he was in shock at how great it came off. We were onstage waiting for the stage crew to drape the sheet over the cage again and he whispered to me, "You're my bitch, so make sure these niggas can see that" referring to onlookers at rehearsal. I nodded yes. We practiced at least 20 times until he was happy with the timing and outcome. He then instructed me to go to his dressing room and wait on him while he finished rehearsing other parts of the show.

(Rob and I at concert in the crowd)

I waited on my man for hours in his dressing room I was ready for him. He finally walked in and asked for me to strip naked and dance for him. He pulled out his penis while on the chair masturbating to me dance. I then straddled him and we began having sex. Kissing to keep me from making noises, until he ejaculated inside me. He wanted to record us having sex but his iPad had a dead battery. Rob had began recording almost every sexual encounter we had and it was uncomfortable for me. One time, I was performing oral sex on him and I opened my eyes to this light from him holding the iPad recording me , I didn't like it but I was too afraid to tell him I didn't want him to do that. Rob was all I had by now. I didn't have a career anymore. My family was in the dark, and I began lying to my best friend about his behavior. I would tell my best friend the bad things and then I would call her back and tell her things were fine, false alarm.

Single Ladies Tour 2012- Rob and I

I didn't want to give up on him because
everyone else had given up on him.
Everyone else had betrayed his trust, or
violated him as a child, or stole money, or
took him to court over greed, and I saw
first hand how paranoid he was. But with

me he was so open and trusting of me, so I had his back no matter how bad it got.

The first night of the tour kicked off well it was a sold out show! He made sure I had plenty of travel cash and lots of freedom. I flew to most of the tour stops while he traveled on his bus. Miami, Houston, Chicago, Milwaukee, you name it we toured!

Our cage skit together was being talked about online a lot. It was very sensual and real for us when the curtain came down you would see our silhouettes kissing and him simulating oral sex on me. Traveling him by bus and me by air built up a lot of anxiousness to see each other at each stop. On a few occasions in the cage he would stick his hand in my pants, saying "it" was his. I was so ready to meet in his dressing room after the show once in Atlanta, but a female R&B singer decided she wanted a piece of my man that night . She was so loud in the hallway, making sure everyone knew she was there. When Rob heard her he walked out into the hallway and greeted her there and kept her away from seeing me. This is the same female he told me was obsessed with him and he once showed me long text threads of her begging to be in his life. He never texted her back. It was sad, he was being nice that night but I remember him saying couldn't stand her loud mouth ass.

She liked the cage skit. I heard her mention it, by then, fans had started uploading the skit on YouTube. With videos from multiple stops up people quickly noticed I was the same girl in every video. It gave away that I was not a random fan he picked from the third row after all!

He and I talked about the Dallas show. I was nervous but anxious because of the radio people that seemed to hate me. He was excited to show me off in my town and it definitely ended up being a huge shock when people saw him grab me onstage and perform our skit ! Point made... I was thinking!

For the next two months it was pure magic between us it was amazing, the closeness, the love, it felt so real. There were dinners in between tour stops where other celebrities would come and hang out. I would always have to turn my chair more towards him and be focused on looking at him talk and only actively be listening to him and not the other men at the table. I forgot not to laugh at a joke one producer told, and he squeezed my hand which was resting on his lap under the table. When dinner ended he slapped me and said I knew why. I did know why, and I was sorry, but he didn't stay angry long.

The second leg of the tour rolled in and we are in NYC for the week of thanksgiving. In the middle of Times Square. We have a beautiful hotel and I have access to all the shopping. Most of the stores are staying open overnight for some sort of a holiday special. I was excited to be in New York. I was about to perform at Madison Square Garden. I thought, how did I go from local radio personality to performing with the biggest star in R&B at Madison Square Garden a year later?! Is this a dream ?

Thanksgiving day comes and he told me that he will come back and get me around 11 AM Because it was a holiday the hotel had no room service that day. I believe there was water, and maybe peanuts in the room. I went the whole day, no food, no phone call from him, nothing! I even pretended with my family that I was having a wonderful Thanksgiving, when they called.

I was pissed, hungry, lonely, and felt disrespected.

I got on my old social media account did some digging around and I saw some people in his camp that posted a photo of a big Thanksgiving feast thrown together for them by Rob. I didn't see Rob again until 11 PM that night. When he came in with no explanation, no nothing.

I was too afraid of him to express my disappointment so I went to sleep silently crying.

Over the next few weeks the tour continued and we ended the tour in Virginia. On the last night of the tour some of the stage crew were planting jokes and gags to make Rob laugh during his performance. It was a tradition that they did on every tour, I was told. On the last show they planted a fake rat inside the cage to scare me. I freaked out and then I laughed really hard, it was really hard to stay in the moment for the audience knowing that they were playing practical jokes on me and Rob. Outside of a couple incidents and me not having a real Thanksgiving I really enjoyed the tour it was the highlight of our relationship. I was able to go home for Christmas to Dallas and he spent the next few weeks after the tour in Vegas as I remember.

The plan was to go back to Chicago after New Year's, back to the Trump Tower where we were living, and pick up where we left off, but when I arrive back he said that he wanted me to move my things into the studio on West Ohio street. He was also moving some of his things in because one of his homes had completely been moved out of, and the Trump Tower was a temporary residence. But he said he wasn't really living there much either and the studio had rooms, a kitchen, TVs, bars, everything you need in a house, it was there. I had a designated room. He had a room with all his things in it too, a bed and a TV with cable. I didn't have a problem with being there it was comfortable and fancy, I thought. I spent most of my time watching a lot of TV. I wasn't allowed to look at reality shows or anything negative. So mainly if I wasn't sitting there listening to him freestyle songs, sing, or have meetings over the phone, I was just inside waiting for him to say it was OK for me to get out that day or go to the mall and see actual people. Someone always had to accompany me if it wasn't him. Once I started living with him at the West Ohio studio he started being even more adamant about making sure I asked before I came out of the room or if I needed to use the restroom. I didn't know it then but two other women were living in different rooms. This was hardly the Playboy mansion style living the media made my life out to be. Unbeknownst to us he was trying ensure we wouldn't bump into each other and add confusion to anything that he was telling any of us.

One evening we were eating from his favorite Chinese spot and he said, "Are you ready to meet the girls"? I said, "yeah" telling him, "If these are people you trust, I trust them too." He said, "Good, good girl I raised them."

Chapter 11
The Pet....

Around March 2013, he called my phone from the other room demanding that I come in his other room and please Daddy I agreed. I walked in and sat in a chair he pointed to. Rob had the iPad set to record. He was naked from waist down. Everything but his shirt was off. I was nude and he was recording me posing for him. In walks a female that he demands to crawl towards me and perform oral sex on me, he told me he raised her, introduced her to me as Jess. He said she was his pet, and a real nasty bitch. That she does everything he says and that he wanted me to pay attention to the things that she will be teaching me. He told me to relax so I won't mess up the recording.

When you think of someone saying they raised anything you think about someone raising animals or raising a child. But I never thought raising in his eyes meant raising someone from a young age to do as he pleases and having sex with him on demand and with other women. I was very confused, the whole first year it was just us. I learned a lot of sexual secrets that he had, like when he had me buy gay porn at one point, and on another occasion one of my male friends loaning me his gay porn for us to view together. Up until then he hadn't invited anyone in our bed, this was the first time.

I don't know where this girl came from and then suddenly it all made sense. He had kept telling me when we met,

"I want to make sure you're ready."

"I want to introduce you to the girls."

"I want to make sure you can handle it."

So I'm thinking THIS is what he was referring to the whole time?! He then joins me and the girl for a sexual threesome. It was awkward. He just started having regular convo soon after it was all over and making her cleanup. We ordered food. One of the runners brought it to the bedroom door. He starts explaining to me how he met her when she was 14. He was very open and candid about it. She was now 27 or 28 so all I kept thinking was, wow here I was semi-intimidated by the girl Sheila and this girl has been around just as long! I then also find out that she and Sheila were actual friends that met him way before me. Rob gives me more of a backstory on how he met her and started raising her around the time he did the soundtrack for the movie Ali. Again I did the math, in my head and I just couldn't believe that he was so open about this but then again I earned his trust.

I didn't like being in this bullshit anymore but I had to make it work , it was the life I chose and felt stuck with.

She seemed nice at first but very robotic. Everything he said she agreed. Everything he laughed at, she laughed at. I just watched her demeanor and she was very well-trained. She had on the clothes he wanted her to wear, just like me. She wore very little make up. Everything was Daddy this, Daddy that.

I wanted to throw up.

It was like I was looking at the person he was trying to turn me into and it disgusted me. I noticed when he would leave the room her demeanor changed towards me. She was no longer laughing, smiling, and being communicative. It was a phony act she had only when he was around to please him. Rob demanded that any girls that he introduced to each other do not get jealous, argue, fight, discuss him to each other without him being around. We were not to talk about anything personal to learn anything about each other's background.

We were allowed to discuss what we were watching on TV, make up, clothes, girly things, food and basics. I didn't like her, she seemed fake and robotic. More importantly she was a threat to me! I thought to myself I had given up too much to let this bitch be someone of importance to him.

But then I couldn't help but think why would she like me either, she had invested over 10 years! I didn't know why he wanted me there if he had all these girls that he raised. What do I add?

My insecurity started kicking in I didn't know what role he wanted me to play in his life. I noticed Jess texting constantly while she was sitting with me. I had been talking to her about going to get my hair done. How the hairdresser mentioned some gossip about Rob not knowing I knew him, and how it made me uncomfortable. She cut me off and said, "Just change hairdressers I don't want to hear anything else about what happened at the hairdresser with you." I looked at her shocked that she flipped into this other person. The innocent baby voice she used around Rob with me was gone and this Chicago urban accent kicked in. Again she kept texting on her phone. Next thing I know Rob opens the door and with his index finger motioning me to come here. My heart sunk because I knew something was going on with her and I was in trouble by the look on his face. He said to me, "Why are you in there talking negative about me? Jess said that you were in there talking negative about me and how you were at the hairdresser discussing me." I couldn't believe what I was hearing. I just started crying and shit because she had completely twisted my words and I wanted to kick her ass for it. But I couldn't explain, Rob was notorious for not allowing anyone to explain themselves. He gets louder and talks over you. Turns out all that time texting on her phone that bitch was texting him lies the whole time! I knew that this girl didn't want me around she had invested too many years and didn't want someone new in his life she had been around through scandals and other women and here I was showing up on tour with him and I'm living with him. As far as she saw it, she had to get rid of me. He slapped me for talking too much. I hated this girl, she lied on me! He took her side and I had no way to prove she was lying. I cried myself to sleep. He was not talking to me over this lie and wouldn't let the runners go get my food orders that I would text them so I didn't eat for a couple of days as punishment. I had water the next day and some pop tarts I found in my bag.

Another time he refused to give me food I had gotten so weak from not eating I passed out in the restroom and woke up cut and bruised. I began texting my best friend very upset about what was

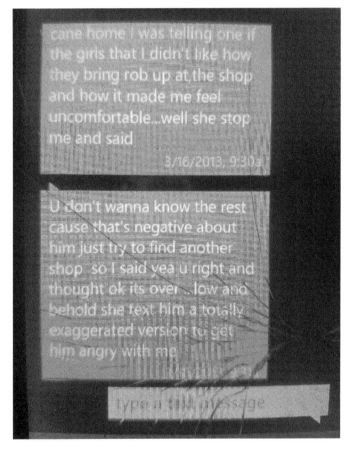

happening. (Text between my best friend and I)

I Was Somebody Before This..

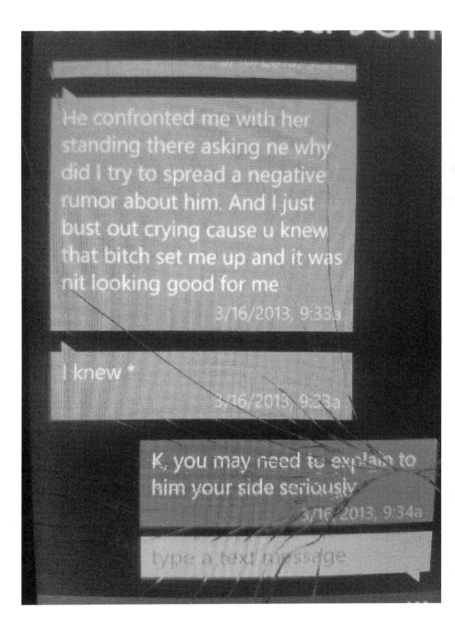

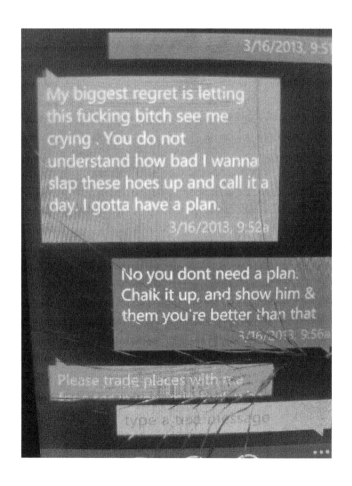

On the third day following the incident with Jess, he came into the room after I had gone to shower and clean up. He says "Sit on Daddy lap I just want to know if you understood what you did wrong." I answered yes and he tells me that Jess is his eyes and ears when he's not around, so don't get mad at her. He says he trained her to tell everything no matter what, and that she's my new sister and that we are a family! She then walks in the room and hugs me. I hated that dirty bitch she caused him to punish me but I also felt relieved because I wanted to get along with people he trusted and I didn't want to be enemies with her since he was so invested in her so much that he would believe her over me. I was hungry, and weak so I just agreed to it. We had dinner in the studio area while he recorded for his Black Panties album. He wanted sex from the both of us and made her go set the room up and to text him when she was done setting it up. He liked Frank Sinatra to be playing, his favorite alcoholic drink, a cigar, and a dim but lit enough room so he could record us. While setting up, another woman walked in and introduced herself, I'll call her Denise. She came into the room and joined the three of us in an orgy where he set up a camera and directed both women to be with each other and instructed them to have sex with me. During this I felt myself gagging while trying to perform oral sex on one the girls and the moment I stood up vomit flew out of my mouth. I cleaned up the mess I made. Disappointed in me, Rob told me to go to my room. For the next two hours, I could hear them through the wall having sex loudly, the three of them. I didn't care about the noises I was just glad I wasn't involved. He came to check on me around 3am and he started playing two songs he wrote asking how I felt about them and that he had me in mind when he wrote them. Both songs made it to his album. One of the songs describes the exact way he courted me and the things he used to say to get me to fly to Chicago to get away from Dallas.

That night after listening to the songs we fell asleep together and I just thought, wow, every time I want to hate him he does something to blow me away.

The next morning he wanted me to accompany Jess to her dentist appointment and told me that we could go get our nails done afterwards and to text him once we get in the car. We had to send a photo of what we are wearing, and at each destination text to make sure he knows where we are. I had to do this even more since the CVS incident when I left the house. It was exhausting trying to remember to text because if each of Jess and I text didn't match up, one of us was going to be in big trouble when we got home . We got our nails done but Rob called my phone and said that Jess told him I was about to get my nails done by a man instead of a woman in the nail shop! I said, "no I wasn't, I can take a photo of the person whose doing them to prove it." He hung up the phone on me. I took the photo and sent it to him and he didn't reply . When we got back home he yelled at me for breaking his rules, which were that men can't do our nails, toes, or massages at shops.. at all! He stated that Jess said I was about to let a man do my nails and when I saw her give me a look, I quickly requested a woman! She lied again! I was furious at her she was setting me up for failure every time she got me alone to tell him fabricated stories. I couldn't trust this person. She was vindictive, manipulative, and evil knowing she can cause me to be starved or beaten just by her lies . She was out to eliminate me. I was new, I was a threat because before me touring and being seen with him nobody was linked to him. She had a mission and it was to make me miserable enough to just leave, even though Rob was abusive she was like an assistant to his abuse. He loved her because she was obedient and loyal and he considered her the trainer, his pet, and his eyes and ears. She didn't want me there. It became torture every week after meeting Jess, I was being slapped , punished with no phone access or starved at this time more than ever. I had lost more weight and everything I knew of my former self at the same time.

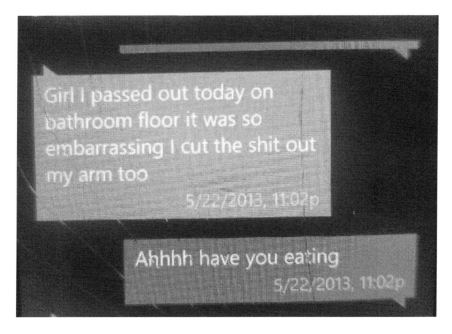

(Text between my friend Toya and I)

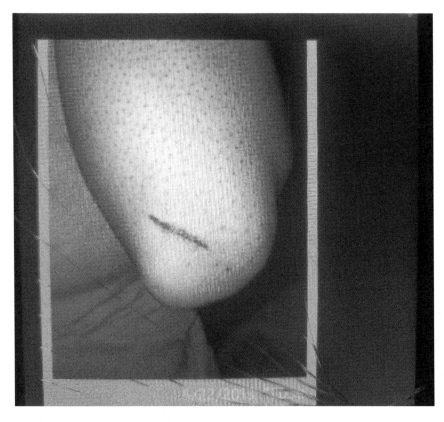

After passing out (March 2013)

Chapter 12
Coachella...And No phone

Yay! On the road again very excited to be traveling all the way from Chicago to LA for Coachella. Rob was making a surprise appearance with Tyler the Creator and only a couple of us knew about it. On the tour bus it ended up taking us a couple days. The bus needed maintenance so we stopped a lot. We ate, stopped at malls, and there was an older woman traveling with us that we had to take back to Vegas. The older lady struck a conversation up with me while Rob was in the back of the bus doing something. She kept asking me where had she seen me before. I didn't really want to answer her question because Rob would've been upset with me for talking too much. She then said, "Wait a minute you were in the cage on the tour right?" The tour had ended at just five months before but I was afraid to answer her. I nodded my head, because she was an older lady, I didn't want her to think I was being rude but what she said next made me want to cry. She said, "I almost couldn't tell it was you, you look so thin compared to when you were in the cage for some reason. I remember you being thicker than that."

All I could think of was wow she has no idea that I lost weight due to being starved, depressed, beaten and slapped around. I didn't have an appetite half the time but when I did want to eat I was on punishment for something Jess likely told Rob about me that was a lie.

I quickly changed the topic there was something on tv so we then started talking about 70s music 80s music. She complimented me on my knowledge. She started asking me my age but when I looked over to my right I saw a Rob peeping through the door in the back of the bus listening to how the conversation will go with me and the older lady that he considered family. I chose my words carefully, but I told her I did radio for a lot of years and I know a lot about music and different genres. Rob walks through the door, sits next to me, and says, "Yeah yeah she did work at the radio station. So tell me something baby if you heard this song right now how would you decide if you guys played it on the radio or not?" I told him I didn't know how most stations did it. But I know where I worked at the time certain songs we will vote on them in a meeting and in my honest opinion if we heard anything by him, if it wasn't with a hip-hop artist, that his songs will be played on our sister station for adult contemporary not our hip-hop station.

This infuriated him. He stood up annoyed with me. He thought I was insulting him calling him old, and outdated, and he immediately told me to shut up, that I was talking to much, and that he didn't ask me for all that information. He called me to the back of the bus away from the older lady. I was already embarrassed when I got to the back of the bus. He grabbed my face and told me that he didn't ever want to hear me talking about my radio job ever again, that I was just trying to draw attention to myself and he's the star of the fucking show not me! I began crying and I told him all I was doing was answering his question and he said, "No you kept talking about shit that didn't have anything to do with what I asked, are you trying to embarrass me bitch?" I told him I would never do anything to make him feel embarrassed, I loved his music. I was just giving him information that he asked for. I kept telling him how sorry I was. He started squeezing my face tighter and tighter, slapped me, and told me when I

walk back in there to shut the fuck up! I felt
so embarrassed and so ashamed. She
was the first person that I was free to talk
to outside of the couple of girls he had
introduced me to and I felt good about
talking about myself and my past and
things that made me feel happy again.
When she saw the look on my face when I
walked out she turned her head as if she
knew what he did and didn't want anything
to do with it . As the bus kept driving I just
kept my head down and turned away. I
couldn't control the tears, they were
coming down my face, I was exhausted it
was May 2013 and In four months I was
going to be at home I just didn't know it at
the time, not yet.

We made it to Coachella I don't know how
she got there but Jess (my worse
nightmare) ended up on the bus I think she
may have flown and then met up with us. I
stayed on the bus at Coachella while he
went and walked to the stage area. I didn't
want to go support him I started hating him

and something inside of me was just over it. I knew when he finished performing at Coachella that he was going to be ready for sex. Three or four times a day he wanted some sort of sex act or just sex so I pretended to be asleep. He didn't care when he came back from performing I had to stand up and praise him. Jess was now on the bus she was hugging him and telling him how great he had done. I was faking it. I wasn't into it my spirits were down. I hate him, I hate him, and that's all I could think of while he sat and talked about the show. I was playing around with my phone I wouldn't look up and make eye contact with him I didn't laugh at him and Jess or participate in the conversation they had. He noticed and he snatched my phone and threw it out the window while the bus was driving. I was just numb I didn't care I wanted to go to sleep and I was hoping that he didn't ask for sex, and he gave Jess a look. She knew what the look meant and started sucking on his penis. He grabbed my face to kiss and when she finished sucking him, he grabbed my waist to sit on his penis.

I faked it.
I hated it,
I hated the environment.
I hated him, and his demands!

I pretended I didn't feel good for over the next day or two. By the time we got back to Chicago I kept faking sick like I had a throat problem or toothache, hoping this would make him leave me alone. I just kept it going for as long as I could. I think after a while he knew I was faking it. I didn't have a phone I just wanted to sleep and be left alone.

June rolled around and I still didn't have a phone so as usual I wasn't getting food. I wasn't worried about eating at this point I just wanted to die.

He would come and check on me. I saw him almost every other day. One afternoon me him and Jess decided to walk to Subway which was about three blocks away from the studio. While we were inside he had me go up to the counter to order the sandwiches. The guy was telling me about a promotion on how to get free sandwiches while I was paying for it. I was listening and nodding my head and I laughed after I asked a question. In my peripheral vision I could see Rob staring at me. When I walked back over to the table to hand the food over and sit he grabbed the food and asked me why was I over there running my fucking mouth. I was supposed to be paying for food not running my fucking mouth! So, instead of us finishing our food there he had me and Jess grab our sandwiches and when we walked out, one of his drivers was already waiting for us by the curb. I guess they knew we were walking and he had already told them to be there to pick us up. Outside Rob was still fussing at me for talking to the worker and slapped me.

All I could think of was wow he was bold enough to do this in front of everybody in broad daylight!

He ordered me to get in the backseat of the car. Jess climbed in and he started telling me to shut up crying, handed Jess money and told her to go shopping with me and to be back home at a certain time-.

Things were getting so bad as far as how he would treat me. He was so bold now with his demands even started asking me to look for other girls to invite to the studio for 'fun' while at the mall. A few different times I booked flights for girls he had found in other cities and they would fly in, entertain us, and go home the next day. He wasn't very generous with them and more than once he would fly them in and decide he didn't like them after all and stand them up the whole day at hotels. He would have the runners take them to the airport the next morning making up lies like "Mr. Kelly has an emergency to leave town. He will be flying you back home and he will contact you next week" That was one of the standard text he would have either me or his runners send girls he didn't end up liking-. But at this point I didn't give a damn how many girls he flew in or what he wanted from me.

I was numb, all I could think back to was what my life was like two years before. How did I get here? How do I get my life back? I started feeling like I was feeding into a sickness like someone with a bad drug habit and I was feeding him a drug, which was in this case was sex. Any type of way that he could get off I helped him do it.

By July I was able to sneak on a hotel computer reactivate my old Facebook account and I asked my best friend to FedEx me a cellphone. I knew he would be asleep if she sent it early in the morning for delivery. She sent it without asking too many questions. The phone was already activated with the phone number on it, and I started focusing the entire month of August how to get the fuck home! I was ready to go!

(Original FedEx package: photo)

Chapter 13

Home

I wasn't being held against my will but I was broken down so much that I felt ashamed of who I had become. I wasn't Kitti Jones the girl that had it all, money, career, and respect from her peers anymore. After having a secret phone, I called some friends back home in Dallas. I had confided in a few friends that I could trust, I didn't go into detail about all the abuse but they knew I wasn't happy anymore . My friend DeeDee remembered seeing me at Christmas after our tour with bruises on my legs. Even though she was a friend I had confided in by then, I lied and told her it was rough sex.

Rob broke me down, stripped me of all I was and groomed me to be another "Pet" in his cult-like environment. I was completely dependent on him in every way and I was trying to think of ways to get my

life back and find a way to leave without it
being a dramatic exit. Although he was
doing these things to me I still felt
protective over him and I didn't want the
world to know what was happening to me
behind closed doors. He had been made
fun of enough and accused of things by
almost everyone from his past. He stayed
in lawsuits it seemed, and still nobody
seemed to care publicly because he had
great music to listen to and amazing stage
presence at his concerts.

I wasn't about to be brushed off as a liar
and groupie so I kept my mouth shut about
what was happening to me. I envied the
"fly in" girls because they could go back to
their lives after a couple nights in Chicago.
I remember when that was me, and I
wanted to turn back time to October of
2011. Before I sold my car and started the
process of trying to please him and move
before quitting my job. I was doing so
much sacrificing of myself, giving up so
much. Fuck loving him, I wasn't even sure

anymore if I even liked the person that I've spent practically two years of my life with?. I was so scared all the time. Hearing an open door made me jump. His voice scared me. I hated his face, his smell, his laugh, the songs ...I hated EVERYTHING and I was on the edge.

Meanwhile I started making plans to go back to Dallas but I didn't have money to start my life over my savings was depleted from loaning out cash to family while I was in Chicago and I used some of it when I had spent time in Atlanta away from Rob. I had just taken a trip to Tampa with one of his "Pets" to visit her family for a graduation and by this time I wasn't having it with his bullshit I was ready to go home.

I started praying more and reading my bible when I was alone. I was crying a lot and begging God to restore my life I asked for forgiveness of the disgusting things I had done that made me feel like I disappointed him, my family, and myself!

Still on the Tampa trip I kept reflecting on a plan to leave when I got back to Chicago. The girl I traveled with was texting him like crazy updating our every move calling him, laughing, happy, and unbothered it was her life and all she knew, but it wasn't mine.

I Was Somebody Before This and I was about to reclaim my fucking life!

Rob started calling me asking why wasn't I texting and calling like the other girl I was with, I got quiet on the phone and said I didn't know(dry and short). I figured since she was face timing you that you could see what was happening and I just didn't think it was a big deal. Rob became furious he started telling me I was a dumb ass bitch (again) and that's why he don't fucking let me do shit no more and he will talk to me when I return back to Chicago. For some reason I wasn't scared I was just ready to get the punishment over with and ignore him until I made a good exit plan .

Praying was working so well it gave me strength, thinking of my mother and how much strength she had at my age inspired me and I didn't put my bible down over the next few weeks. Rob noticed and so did Jess. They seemed uncomfortable about it because I left my bible on a chair in her room one day and she hid my bible for two weeks. We were not allowed to communicate with each other independent of Rob so I kept asking Rob to have her give it to me and one day I heard a noise at my door and it was someone sliding my bible under the door. It was her. How disgusting can you be to hide someone's bible?

One evening in mid August (2 weeks before my exit) we were in Robs room watching tv, when he started eating crab legs and laughing at the show on tv. I hadn't eaten the entire day and I was starved. I could tell Jess was as well. We had to wait on him to tell us we could order food or eat. We also had to thank him for giving us food each time as well. You would assume eating shouldn't be looked at as privilege but to Rob, he insisted we thanked him. I glanced over at him and then looked back at the tv. He said "Don't watch me eat, " I noticed Jess was stiff watching tv and I said, "I wasn't watching you, I just looked at you." He motioned to kick my thigh but missed then slapped me for talking back and told me to get out the room. I stared at him with anger this time ready to fight back. He stood up and grabbed me from behind, walked me out, took me in my room, and started yelling at me about the Tampa trip pushing my head really hard against the wall. All I remember was I was ready to kill this mother fucker and swung back at him this time. I fell and he kept kicking and slapping me. He walked out and I went without food that night and the next day.

I was now at the end of my tolerance level. I thought back to a night in March when I contemplated killing myself or him. I text a long time friend who said if I wanted to come back to Dallas quietly without anyone in my business I could stay at her house while I figured things out. I was grateful to have her offer me a place to come. I wasn't up for explaining why I was back in town to anyone or what went down. I just wanted out of Chicago so I had a great idea planned.

After the third day following the fight I text him and said "Hey Daddy I'm sorry about disappointing you and I'm still trying to learn things, please forgive me, and if you will please allow me to take my son school shopping in a couple of days he is starting high school and I just want to do that and come back afterwards." He replied " Hey baby, Daddy forgives you and yes you can, how much is the flight and what do you need for shopping? I said, "I haven't looked at the flight yet, I wanted your permission first," just trying to make him feel in charge of me still, "but I probably will need $4500." He said "OK one of the guys will slide the envelope under your door with the cash in it but text the flight info to the runner so they can pay it separately." I got scared because it seemed so easy, I started shaking while packing my things. Rob slept hard during the day in a separate room and I was glad about it because he was too sexual and demanded sex and oral even when I was half asleep not wanting to, so the nights he wasn't around me, it was perfect sleep and peaceful.

Planning my flight I had to book it as round trip so it wouldn't look suspicious. I sent my desired flight info and they booked me to leave around 11am. Before I left he checked my bags to see what I had packed removing anything that indicated I was going to party like heels , extra handbags, dressy clothes etc. All I had was a few basic outfits and mostly sweatpants in two suitcases and I had a Gucci bag he bought me earlier that year

around Valentine's Day. I didn't care that I
was leaving my entire wardrobe behind
and personal belongings. I just wanted my
life back! I was fucking over him and his
weird ass bitches who stuck around longer
than the two years I had. I remember Jess
walking in my room to grab something
from the bar area for Rob my last night
there. She had this smirk on her face I
would never forget, it took every part of me
to resist attacking her for contributing to
my living hell the last 9 months. But then I
thought…she's sick. She's been
brainwashed by this man and this is all
she's known and done so of course she's
determined to eliminate everyone he
becomes smitten by. I turned off my anger
and sympathized because at least I was
going back to a place and I could rebuild. I
had family, friends and one hell of a
resume and good credit to get my shit
back on track. These girls couldn't say the
same .

The next morning I said goodbye to Rob I was crying because I knew it was over, he didn't . I took photos of a few things before I left like the puppies and the building. When I got outside, I hopped in a taxi with my things and arrived at the airport. While waiting on my flight I kept getting cold feet. I wanted to go back to the studio. I was more afraid what I would face in Dallas than back with Rob. I didn't want my family asking me why I was back, why was I so skinny (now at 107 pounds and frail).
 Nor did I want to hear my old colleagues making fun of me on the radio as they had done several times before. I was scared at the airport. All these thoughts going through my head. I went into the bathroom stall and cried so hard my contacts slid out. I tried calling Rob and he didn't answer, he must've been asleep. I boarded the flight finally and I thought please hurry and get in the sky so I won't change my mind because if he calls back before take off I'm getting off this flight.....

I landed in Dallas around 2:30 pm on a Thursday right before Labor Day weekend. What happened to me over the couple of years being back in Dallas was shocking, causing me to wish I had never returned at times, and it wasn't the last of me and Rob.

Chapter 14
Restoration

I was so happy to be home! The first couple of days I took my son shopping and was so happy to be free of the abuse and control. I had gotten so use to not eating in my relationship that I barely remembered to eat now that I had the freedom to. Rob kept calling my phone because I was supposed to be texting him my moves, showing what I was wearing and constantly giving updates. He didn't know when he last saw me it was literally the last. Or at least I thought so. He thought I was getting back on the flight back to Chicago that Saturday after taking my son shopping but had me fucked up this time.

I finally text him to say I was safe at home and that I wasn't returning, and quickly powered that phone off, too scared of his reaction. I got a cheap prepaid phone and kept the power off on that iPhone because his calls were giving me anxiety attacks. I started gradually forcing myself to eat to gain weight back because I had gotten tired of people asking me why was I so thin. I was known for having a nice frame (this is why Rob loved me in the cage silhouette) and I was dramatically smaller. I didn't want to explain why, so I said "All that traveling and going all the time, you forget to eat." Another excuse I had was I stopped eating bad foods. After being back and staying with a childhood friend a month I got my own apartment. Rent was high but I was busy trying to prove to anyone who knew I was back in town that nothing had changed! Now that my ex-husband had returned full time from Italy he was living in our old house. With my son now living in the states again he was also ready to just physically live with me. His dad started giving a monthly amount of money that we agreed on. I had gotten a job at a auto finance company and was getting back on my feet. All within a month I had gotten a place, job, and new car. I was moving fast but I wasn't going places where I could possibly run into anyone that worked at my old job or knew about my dealings with Rob.

I didn't have a rehearsed answer to give yet.

I didn't want any old coworkers to get on air and make fun of my size or make assumptions as to why I was back home either . I hated some of the people at my old job because they had the power to persuade opinions because of the platform they had. Hundreds of thousands of people heard them make fun of me in gossip segments over the years, since my departure, and I wasn't about to give them another reason to humiliate me again.

Although I started being content with a regular job and being low key, I had gotten a bright idea to go set up an interview with my old station's competitor, another hip hop station. I thought yes, this will be good revenge! I would have gotten my old life back all within a 4-6 week timeframe if I joined another station. I made a call and tried my damnest to be the old Kitti I was known for. I got the guy in charge on the phone and he was open to speaking with me that day! I drove up to that station excited that this could work so I mustered up the confidence and walked into the building. The guy in charge greeted me and we went into his office where another manager joined him for the interview. Immediately he began asking me what happened at 97.9 and why did I quit. But I wasn't dumb. I knew, he knew I was living with R. Kelly those two years and we toured. I got nervous but I said, I sent them an email resigning due to some family issues that would've prevented me from fulfilling my duties etc… which was the true email I sent…. and explained to him that this "ruffled some feathers", that's behind me and I am living back in the area and I think I can bring a lot to your team. He looked over at the other guy in the room and they started asking me about rumors they heard and that how could they be so sure that if R. Kelly didn't show up if I wouldn't just quit there too?

I knew it! I knew people in this business were not going to give me a fair chance after Rob. I was offended and embarrassed. Instead of explaining, I thanked him for his time and told him I understood his concern. I was defeated.

He said to give him a call to talk again. I had a nervous smile on my face and stood up to walk out I left out shaking so bad that I couldn't manage to start my car once I was in the lot. Here I was trying to restore all I had lost and this was a huge blow! I became very depressed over that meeting and to top it off someone that worked there sent me a message saying they basically never had good intentions, just wanted some "tea". I planned to NEVER be around anything related to both stations or support any events they had and asked my friends and family to do the same. My career was gone in Dallas. I had to accept it.

At the new job I hated it, it wasn't my passion at all and they were nit picking over the dumbest things but because it was low key and nobody recognized me and I didn't have to answer questions before I was ready regarding my past, I made this work for now. It was a nice check to keep me on track with bills but a huge difference from radio money and very humbling. I had asked God before coming home to get me back here and allow me to restore my life, so the money didn't matter, I was happy to be surviving without Rob.

There were days at my desk I would just start crying in silence trying to make sure nobody saw me. Tears would just roll down my face because I was still hiding everything from everyone and dealing with a lot internally. One of my coworkers saw me crying and wrote scriptures on sticky notes. Without asking what's wrong or being nosey he would just place them on my desk for encouragement. That always stuck with me and til this day he's my male best friend, with no hidden agenda and never tried anything with me. My best friend Toya was the shit at keeping me focused on the good, she was cooking dinners and having movie nights at her house helping me stay positive and taking me to church with her. I told her the truth about most of what happened and she was furious that I didn't say anything so I could come live with her before it had gotten that bad. She felt guilty for not flying up there to get me. We are the same age, birthdays just days apart and we met in 5th grade, she was so overprotective at this point because she knew how people were talking about me and how they didn't know the real story . She kept me on point, not feeding into rumors, and just giving God my issues.

Just as things seemed to be calm, driving home from work one day, listening to the radio, I started hearing promos about R.Kelly coming to town for a party at a nightclub. I became so nervous in the car that I had to pull over and use a bathroom at a gas station (out of my character because I have issues with public restrooms). I thought to myself what the fuck is he coming here for? He never showed up in the past, EVER for just a club appearance. He would do appearances if he was on tour as an afterparty but not just a standalone appearance!! I knew he was going to get me when he found me so I was scared again! Scared because of how I left. Scared because I knew too much, and he knew this!

I wanted to get my emotions together stat! So I called him anonymous to play things down. He didn't answer the phone. I waited a few minutes to make sure that if I called him with my number showing that I would be ok with him having my number and what may come with it. I got home and started stressing about this like why is this mother fucker coming here out of all places? I called my sister and told her he was coming and she was like, "Oh cool I wanna go with you if you go." She didn't my secret. She didn't know what he had done to me. She assumed like many that it was a mutual breakup. Suddenly I thought THAT'S IT!! I can call him, play it cool and ask him if me and my family can come see him at his club gig! I called unblocked and he answered fast. My heart sunk, his voice still had an effect on me. I said, "Hello… Daddy can you hear me" with my voice shaking, he says "Hey baby, guess you're not mad no more, you good?" I replied, "Yes I'm good Daddy, and I'm not mad I just wanted to come be with my family cause it was a lot going on and I didn't think you would understand." He said "OK cool, I will be out there next week and I'll bring you the stuff you left here. Call me tonight around 8 or 9 ok, I'm in the middle of something. You love Daddy still?" I smiled inside, I was feeling so glad he wasn't in a rage or calling me bitches and

threatening me, so I answered " Yes
Daddy I love you, call you later."

He and I kept in touch for a week the
conversations were positive and he didn't
seem to have any animosity about leaving
and he was thrilled about his new album
Black Panties coming out. I knew most of
the songs already because he recorded
them and played the tracks over and over
for a year at home . I was telling him how
proud I was of him. I wanted him to feel
secure that I wasn't going to tell anyone
what happened to me, or file charges, or
sue him, thinking he would leave me
alone. The day he arrived in town he
asked me to meet him at a certain time on
his bus to get my things and that my sister
and cousin could come with me. Shortly
before I was to arrive to meet him, he said
"Come by yourself so we can talk baby". I
said "ok", and he said " I love you, tell
them they can come to the show with you
though." I bet he thought I cared about all
the clothes, shoes, bags, and personal

items I left behind enough to return at some point but I didn't give a damn about material things enough to go back into that hell I left.

My guards were down because he sounded fine, I loved that we were talking and there was no beef. I got cute, washed my car, and drove to meet him on his bus parked in a hotel parking lot. I walked onto his bus, nobody but him was around. All hell broke loose, he started hitting me and choking me telling me I wasn't getting shit back and never fuck with him like that, swinging on me and in a rage. His voice was high pitched, yelling "do I look like I'm a stupid nigga to you bitch!" I was injured, but got away. I ran into my car trying not to make a scene.

He had put fear back in me again and moving forward I was going to stay silent. It had been too much to deal with and I wasn't ready for anyone to know, and they wasn't going to believe me any damn way!

I lied and told my sister and cousin that Rob and I had an argument and I wasn't going to the show and I suggested we go elsewhere to celebrate the holidays and being off work.

Over the next three years I lived in fear and shame hiding myself again from things I used to live to do, looking at old photos of before I left to Chicago made me cry because I had a happy look in my eyes. Now I started taking less photos of myself people who knew me saw the difference in me. I wasn't confident anymore and couldn't fake it much with a smile so I hated how photos looked of me because I knew the depression I was suffering with. Two and a half years go by, barely dating, and when I did, I dated just to cover my issues. Nobody was good for me at all. Either using me, or being too aggressive with wanting my time. I moved to another area far away from my old apartment and closer to work. I was a hermit and avoided crowds and meeting new men or people at all. I wasn't happy and 2016 was ending I got on my knees to ask God some questions…

I prayed; God, why me, I've done right by people in my life except for being an adulterer and I repented for that, I've made things right with family members that I had long feuds with and I felt I had suffered enough, and if more suffering was coming I wanted him to just take me, in my sleep, I was tired.

I started just "existing" and not living, the same way I remembered people in my old neighborhood doing, as a kid with dreams, I never wanted to be that. I was asking God if he wanted me here then to show me why I went through the things I did and to make it al make sense to me. Two days later after Christmas Day 2016, I received a message in my social media account inbox from a parent who said she needed my help, that her daughter was a victim of Rob's and that she was told a lot about my situation with him, and heard that I was able to get away, and to please contact her.

I got scared wondering how she found me and why me? He dated tons of people why ask me for help? What can I do?

She then sent me a message and a photograph that dropped my jaw and it wasn't over yet with Robert Kelly, or the radio station .....

I Am Still Somebody..... Spring of 2018.

Kitti Jones
www.spytheproject.com
Stop Protecting Your Abuser
Visit to share your inspirational stories and resources to help someone that may not have the courage to stand up to their abuser yet.

Made in the USA
Columbia, SC
01 October 2021

46515309R00087